ABSOLUTE BEGINNERS

Irish Tenor Banjo

T0080404

HAL•LEONARD®

Published by
Hal Leonard,

Exclusive Distributors:
Hal Leonard,
7777 West Bluemound Road,
Milwaukee, WI 53213
Email: info@halleonard.com

Hal Leonard Europe Limited,
42 Wigmore Street, Marylebone,
London WIU 2RY
Email: info@halleonardeurope.com

Hal Leonard Australia Pty. Ltd.
4 Lentara Court, Cheltenham,
Victoria 9132, Australia
Email: info@halleonard.com.au

Order No. AM998734
ISBN: 978-1-84938-276-2
This book © Copyright 2015 Hal Leonard

Written by Éamonn Coyne.
Edited by David Bradley and Adrian Hopkins.
Music processed by Paul Ewers Music Design.
Book design by Chloë Alexander.
Photography by Matthew Ward.
Photograph on page 21 courtesy of Clodagh Kilcoyne/Getty Images.

Music recorded and mixed by Jonas Persson and Imogen Hall
Mastered by Jonas Persson
Banjo by Éamonn Coyne
Guitar accompaniments by Kris Drever

*Éamonn Coyne uses D'Addario strings and plays a
David Boyle banjo.*

www.eamonncoyne.com
www.daveboylebanjos.com
www.halleonard.com

Contents

Introduction

Welcome to *Absolute Beginners Irish Tenor Banjo*. This book will hopefully launch you into the world of the tenor, or four-string, banjo – specifically, a banjo tuned to GDAE (commonly referred to as EADG) as when used playing traditional Irish and Scottish music. Tricks and tips will be passed on to the beginning player to lay down a nice path to advanced playing. I think it is important that all beginners start out properly and, with enough practice and playing, become as good as they can.

There is also plenty of advice and techniques covered in the book which should be useful to intermediate and advanced players too.

There are many excellent articles written about the history of the banjo – be it the three-, four-, five- or six-string variety – and they differ in opinions making the exact origin of the instrument obscure, but the general view is that the banjo, or at least the idea behind the banjo, was introduced to the world from Africa. The prototype to the instrument we know today most likely took shape in seventeenth-century America when African slaves made instruments by adding a neck with strings to drums (gourds or wooden shallow rims). These strings were gut and the coverings of the drums were animal skin or vellum.

From there the banjo went in many directions – too many to go into here – but suffice to say that it lead to a four-string instrument which was used for many different types of music. The most popular tuning for this "tenor" banjo was (and possibly still is in all but traditional Irish music) CGDA, where the open A is the same as an open A on the violin and commonly tuned to 440Hz.

What has come to be known as the "Irish banjo", which has more to do with tuning than anything else, has its roots in the same place. The popularisation of the tenor instrument, to which this "Irish banjo" title refers, was by the late, great, and much missed Dubliner Barney McKenna. Throughout the 1960s and 1970s, he made the tenor banjo, which he tuned to GDAE, popular as a member of The Dubliners. This tuning is an octave below the fiddle.

I play this GDAE-tuned tenor banjo and without Barney, neither I nor many of my colleagues in banjo music would be around today. He was the "papa bear" of the Irish banjo and one of the nicest, most knowledgeable, and informative people you could ever meet!

Some further reading on the history of the banjo:

- www.standingstones.com/banjo.html
- www.blarneystar.com/BANJO_030912X.pdf
- www.en.wikipedia.org/wiki/Banjo
- www.banjohangout.org/article/7

Parts of the Tenor Banjo

Most of the parts are also known by different names.

Headstock with four tuning pegs
Many different designs exist but all have the same purpose: to tune the strings by varying their tensions. The strings are wrapped around the **tuning pegs**.

Nut
Made of a piece of bone or plastic, the **nut** has four grooves which hold the strings, evenly spaced.

Strings
The tenor banjo has four strings of differing 'gauges' (thicknesses) and run the length of the instrument.

Neck and fretboard with frets
The neck of the tenor banjo has frets along a hardwood fretboard. The placement of a finger along those frets varies the length of the string and therefore the pitch of the note produced by plucking the string. There are usually markings (inlays) at intervals along the fretboard as reference points.

Pot, tone ring, head, stretcher band, flange
The neck is joined to what is called the "pot", which is a round cylinder commonly made of wood, on top of which is generally placed a **tone ring**. The tone ring often greatly contributes to how good a particular banjo sounds or how well it rings out, as does the materials and construction of the pot. On top of the tone ring is a drum head – also simply called a "skin" – made of plastic but originally, as with most drum heads, this would have been vellum or animal skin. The **stretcher band** holds the head in place, and it is held on by "J-bolts", which are attached to the **flange**. In this way the head can be tightened or loosened.

Bridge
This is often made of two pieces of wood: a softwood base with a hardwood top with grooves, corresponding to those in the nut, to retain the strings. As with most banjo parts, these come in all shapes and sizes.

Resonator
Often called simply the "back", the **resonator** is used to project the pot's sound forwards.

Tailpiece
This is what anchors the strings beyond the bridge; again, these come in many varieties.

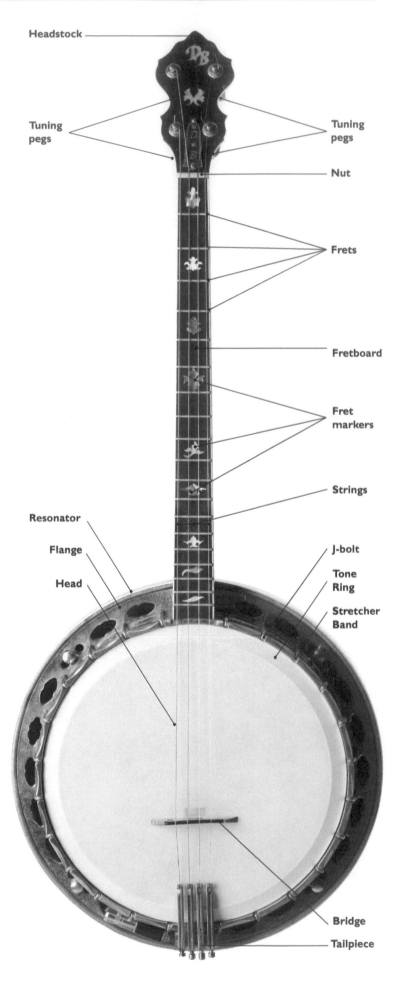

Strings

The tenor banjo has four strings and, as far as we deal with in this book, they are tuned to GDAE. The strings go from heavier to lighter from the bottom/thickest string (G) to the top/lightest string (E). Strings are measured in tenths of an inch by their diameter (thickness) and are referred to as ".11s" or ".34s". The tuning is sometimes referred to as EADG.

The strings themselves are most likely to be single guitar strings of the appropriate gauges, but many companies and musical instrument stockists put sets together to suit particular needs. There are many varieties of strings available on the market and people use different gauge selections for their strings.

string	tuning	type	diameter/ gauge	'called'	D'Addario code
1st	E	plain steel	0.011"	11	PL011
2nd	A	plain steel	0.017"	17	PL017
3rd	D	phosphor bronze	0.026"	26	EXPPB026
4th	G	phosphor bronze	0.034"	34	EXPPB034

I find that coated bronze strings give me a brighter tone for longer from the bottom strings, but this is simply personal taste.

Tuning (GDAE)

The highest, thinnest string, is called the first string and it is tuned to what is referred to as a high E (also written E'). The second string is tuned to an A. The third string is tuned to a D. The bottom, thickest string is called the fourth string and is tuned to a low G (also written G').

Track 1: E A D G banjo strings in tune

The strings are tightened to increase the pitch and loosened to decrease the pitch. The direction of higher or lower is dependant on what tuning peg system your banjo uses.

Tuning to a Piano Keyboard

The strings of a tenor banjo are tuned in fifths, which means that the strings differ in pitch by five tones (see tuning figure below). This means you can tune the strings to one another if one of the strings is in tune and the intonation (tuning of the frets as you move up the neck) of your banjo is good. This is what is known as relative tuning.

The pitch A can be obtained from a piano, tuning fork, pitch pipes, or another in-tune instrument, to which the A (second) string of the banjo can be tuned. The E (first or top) string can then be tuned to the seventh fret of the A string. The seventh fret of the D (third) string can be tuned to the open A string. Once the D string is in tune, the seventh fret of the G (fourth or bottom) string can be tuned to the open D string.

Track 2: tuning of banjo strings at 7th fret

Banjo Tuning

For performing and recording, most players use electronic tuners, which come in all shapes and sizes. These vary from chromatic tuners with built-in microphones, to clip-on tuners which clip onto the headstock, to pedal tuners for use with instruments with built-in pick-ups. The clip-on type is very common but, if this is the route you go, it is worth getting a good one that fits your headstock well.

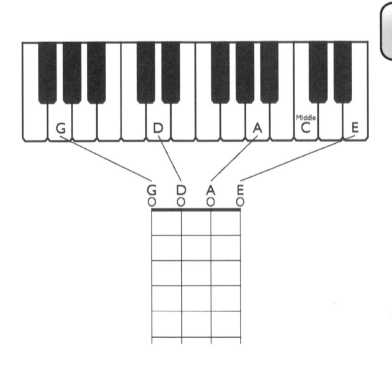

Holding the Tenor Banjo

There are many different ways to hold the tenor banjo but in general it comes from the same ideas: be comfortable and get the best sound. I can only speak for myself and what suits me.

The banjo is sat between, and touching, both legs and sloped back slightly into the body. The neck is held at about a thirty-degree angle and pointing slightly away from the body. The right forearm rests against the rim of the stretcher band with little or no contact with the head/skin, with the side of the palm only lightly touching the strings behind the bridge, if even touching at all.

The exact position is determined by where the plectrum makes contact with the strings in order to produce the best sound – not too close to the bridge (which produces a tinny/tight sound) or too close to the neck (which produces too soft/loose sound).

▼ Here the position of the plectrum makes contact with the strings in order to produce the best sound

▼ Too close to the bridge (which produces a tinny/tight sound)

For me on my banjo, the best position is as follows:

- the bottom of the resonator in my lap about six inches from my torso, the neck at an angle of about thirty degrees off parallel, and the top of the resonator leaning back against my body under my chest.
- the stretcher band rim touching my forearm about three inches from my wrist and about one inch above the tailpiece.
- the anchor point is where the rim touches my forearm.
- the plectrum touches the strings about two inches in front of the bridge.

But remember this is not an exact science as everyone is different and banjo designs differ greatly.

Remember to be relaxed but also remember good posture to ensure the whole process isn't going to ruin your back or the rest of your body. Also, if you are too tense this will get into your playing and that, in turn, may well be tense too. Try all this out with your own banjo and see what feels and sounds right.

▼ Too close to the neck (which produces too soft/loose sound)

As with strings (and of course banjos themselves) there are many, many types of **plectrums** (or "picks") available in all shapes and sizes made from all kinds of material. Again, choosing one usually comes down to personal preference; I use a Jim Dunlop nylon plectrum with a thickness of .60 mm (the medium-grey one – not too dark grey or not too light grey!). This is what I have always used and it suits my playing. For me it is just hard enough, flexible enough, and pointy/ rounded enough without being too much the other direction in any of those categories.

How the plectrum is held is, again, a personal thing but there are some general pointers. I believe general consensus is that it should be held pretty perpendicular and at a slight angle to the strings to aid easy movement when moving between the strings. How it is held in the fingers is a more personal thing.

I hold it lightly/loosely between my thumb and first finger with a bit of my second finger on the plectrum too. Again, this is how I have always done it so it is most likely a comfort thing. The rigidity of the hold is quite important: too tight and it is harder to play fluently; too loose and it can fall out of your hand! The best way I can describe it is that the plectrum should 'give' a little when the strings are plucked.

Picking

The motion for the plectrum is predominantly down-strokes followed by up-strokes. To move between the strings you have to move your hand up and down and the plectrum is just an extension of your hand when you are playing. However, I am not obsessed with everything being down, up, down, up etc. The most important reason for this up-and-down motion of the plectrum is that it enables you to pick the tunes more fluidly (and faster in some cases).

The position of the plectrum on the strings relative to the bridge depends on your banjo. It is about getting the best sound from the string (*see* Holding the Tenor Banjo, page 8). On my banjo, this is when the plectrum touches the strings about two inches in front of the bridge.

Because of the angles involved in holding the instrument and rotation of the wrist, the movement of the plectrum is also at a slight angle to the bridge. This angle relative to the bridge means that the plectrum is slightly closer to the bridge for the E string but slightly further away for the G string. This angle makes little difference to the sound as it is only slight.

Exercises using open strings with backing track
Try playing the open strings from the G to the E
playing each note a few times in succession.
With all down-strokes of the plectrum play:

Gı	**G**ı	**G**ı	**G**ı	(fourth string – bottom, thickest, lowest)
D	**D**	**D**	**D**	(third string)
A	**A**	**A**	**A**	(second string)
E'	**E'**	**E'**	**E'**	(first string – top, thinnest, highest)

Listen for the best sounds the plectrum makes relative
to the bridge position for each note.
Start at about two inches and see where you get to.

 **Track 3: playing open strings
(all down strokes)**

Next, when you have a good idea of where to
position the plectrum, try introducing the down, up,
down, up motion I mentioned earlier (to aid smooth,
fluid movement between the strings).

Starting with a down-stroke of the plectrum –
followed by an up stroke – followed by a down
stroke – followed by an up-stroke, play:

Gı (down)	**G**ı (up)	**G**ı (down)	**G**ı (up)

Then repeat for:

D (down)	**D** (up)	**D** (down)	**D** (up)

Then repeat for:

A (down)	**A** (up)	**A** (down)	**A** (up)

Then repeat for:

E' (down)	**E'** (up)	**E'** (down)	**E'** (up)

This should all be repeated over and over to get fluid
motion of the plectrum on the strings.

 **Track 4: playing open strings
(down-up-down-up strokes)**

How did you get on?
Are you ready for some more notes?

Basic Music Theory

Tablature

Before we go any further, let's talk about basic music notation. All examples in this book are written in standard music notation and tablature.

Tablature, commonly referred to as **TAB**, is a form of musical notation in which frets (instead of notes) are indicated on lines representing the strings. There are four lines for tenor banjo TAB. The top line corresponds to the first string, or open E. A "5" placed on the top line means to play at the fifth fret on the E string, which is the note A.

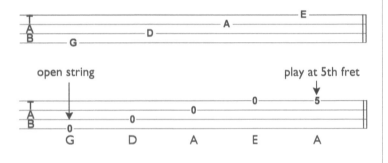

Standard Music Notation

Tablature only tells us where to play a note. To know *when* and *how long* to play a note, we use **standard music notation**. In standard notation, notes are written on a **staff** of five lines and four spaces. At the beginning of the staff is a **treble clef**, also known as a "G" clef because the curl of the clef passes through the G line. This clef determines what notes will be on the lines and spaces.

Notes are named consecutively using the first seven letters of the alphabet (from A through G) continuing infinitely in both directions. There are seven **scale degrees**, meaning there are seven notes before you reach the note you started with. An octave is the distance from A to the next A, or B to the next B, and so on.

Between all **natural** notes there are two frets, with two exceptions: between B and C, and E and F, where there is only a one-fret difference. In relation to a keyboard, there is no "black" key between these sets of notes. Therefore, when we play an open-string G on the banjo, the note A is located at the second fret, B is located at the fourth fret, and C is located at the fifth fret, since the distance between B and C is only one fret. That is why when we tune we place our finger at the seventh fret (D) to match the adjacent open D string.

Notes for all five lines starting from the bottom are **E – G – B – D – F**. A phrase to help remember the notes is: **Every Good Boy Does Fine**.

The spaces between the notes also have names: **F – A – C – E**. Remember this by saying, **"In a space there is a face."**

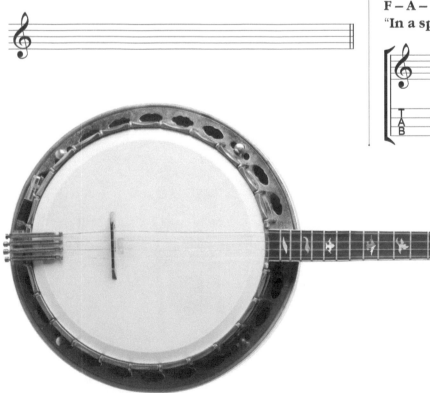

When you add the lines and spaces together, you get the musical alphabet.

Starting from the bottom line of the staff, the sequence of notes is **E – F – G – A – B – C – D – E – F.**

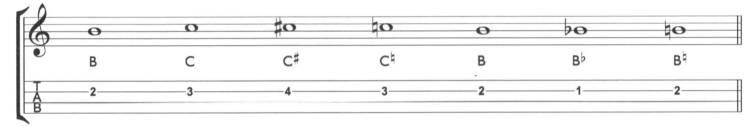

Accidentals are signs used to tell us whether to raise or lower a note by a *half step*, or one fret. There are three types of accidentals:

♯ (sharp)—raises a note by a half step (one fret)
♭ (flat)—lowers a note by a half step (one fret)
♮ (natural)—cancels sharps and flats

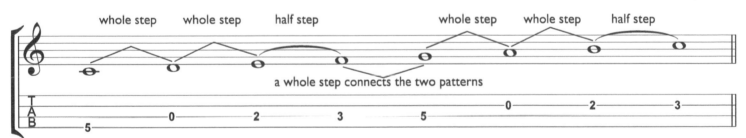

If a *half* step equals one fret, then a whole step equals two frets. Therefore, there are whole steps between all natural notes except between B and C, and E and F, which are separated by half steps.

The **major** scale is comprised of two equal sequences of notes connected by a whole step. The pattern is as follows: whole step–whole step–half step; a whole step connects the next pattern: whole step–whole step–half step.

<figure>
whole step   whole step   half step   whole step   whole step   half step

a whole step connects the two patterns

TAB: 5 — 0 — 2 — 3 — 5 — 0 — 2 — 3
</figure>

Key Signatures

Key signatures tell us exactly that—what key the piece is in. Key signatures are notated at the beginning of the staff after the clef with either sharps (♯) or flats (♭).

The three keys we will be dealing with in this book are G, D, and A.

The key of G has one sharp—F♯, which means that whenever and wherever you play an F it will always be sharp.

The only time it will not be sharp in the key of G is when a natural sign (♮) is placed directly in front of the note.

The key of G has one sharp—F♯:

The key of D has two sharps—F♯ and C♯:

The key of A has three sharps—F♯, C♯, and G♯:

Rhythmic Notation

Music is divided into **measures**, which are separated by **barlines**. Double barlines show the end of a section, and **final barlines** mark the end of the tune.

A note's **rhythmic value** is determined by its shape, stem, and flag: Whole notes (o) equal four beats and are counted 1-2-3-4. Half notes (𝅗𝅥) equal two beats, and two half notes equal one whole note. A quarter note (♩) equals one beat. Two quarter notes equal a half note and four quarter notes equal a whole note.

An eighth note (♪) is equal to half a beat. Two eighth notes equal a quarter note, four eighth notes equal a half note, and eight eighth notes equal a whole note.

Eighth notes are counted with "+" or as "ands" (1+2+3+4+), and can be grouped together by beams.

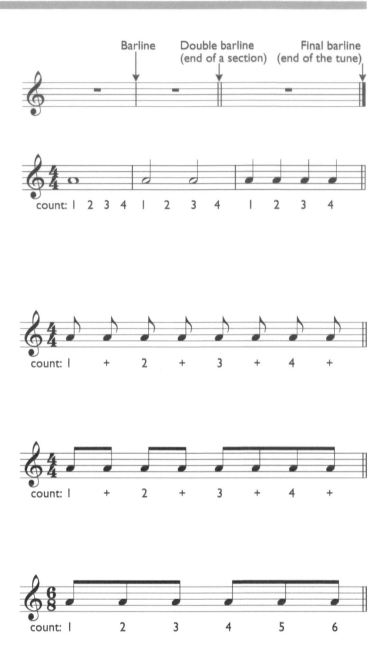

For each note there is an equivalent **rest**.
A rest is a period of silence that takes the place of a note.

For example, a quarter-note rest equals one beat of silence.

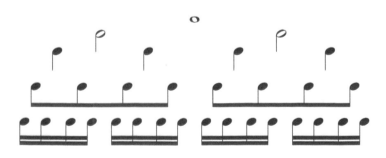

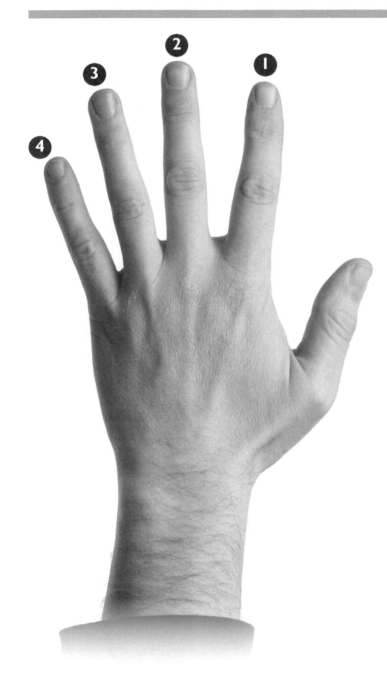

Left-Hand Technique

There are two common systems associated with the tenor banjo in relation to what finger plays what note ("fingering") – possibly described as either being connected with the fiddle/mandolin or with the cello/guitar.

Mine – which is based on the fiddle fingering – is as follows:

First finger plays the first and second frets
Second finger plays third and fourth frets
Third finger plays fifth fret
Fourth finger plays sixth and seventh frets

Some people use the third finger for the fourth fret and the fourth finger for the fifth fret. This works really well for some people, just not for me. To my mind I am out of fingers at that stage. I sometimes will stray from this depending on the key of the tune but this will be connected with the stretch involved.

The positioning of the thumb comes down to one of comfort for me – not too far around towards the top of the neck, and not too far towards the bottom of the neck.

My hand tends to be anchored by my thumb, which doesn't move a lot except when playing a few notes in particular, but more of that later.

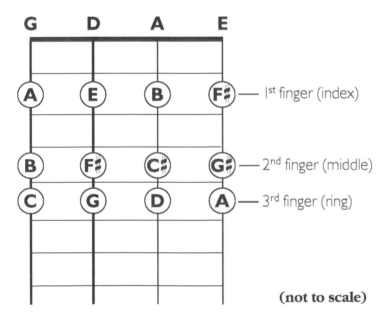

(not to scale)

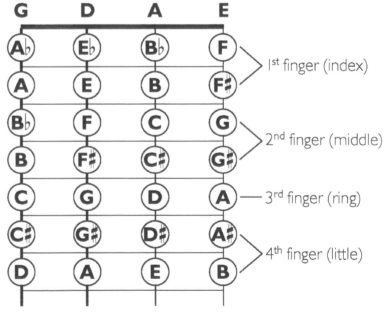

The D String

We will now play the notes on the D string in the key of D and demonstrate what fingers we use to play them. The notes are:

Exercise 1

D   E   F#   G

And they are played as:

D
open D (third) string

E
first finger on second fret

F#
second finger on fourth fret

G
third finger on fifth fret

Maybe try this system:

1   Finger the notes by just using your left hand (imagine you have played the open D!);
2   then play them with your right-hand thumb;
3   then introduce the plectrum.

 Track 5: Exercise 1 with plectrum (all down)

Now you can try playing **Exercise 2**:

D   E   F#   G   F#   E   D

Use the same fingers on the way back down to the D and try it using the same system as before – left hand only, then with thumb, then with plectrum.

 Track 6: Exercise 2 with plectrum (all down)

The next thing to try is playing **Exercise 2** now with the plectrum moving down, up, down, up etc.

 Track 7: Exercise 2 with plectrum (down, up, etc.)

We will now move to the A string and play the notes on the A string in the key of A.
The notes are:

Exercise 3

And they are played as:

A
open A (second) string

B
first finger on second fret

C♯
second finger on fourth fret

D
third finger on fifth fret

Again maybe try this:
1 Finger the notes by just using your left hand;
2 then play them with your right-hand thumb;
3 then introduce the plectrum.

 Track 8: Exercise 3 with plectrum (all down)

Now you can try playing **Exercise 4**:

Use the same fingers on the way back down to the A and try it using the same system as before – left hand only, then with thumb, then with plectrum.

 Track 9: Exercise 4 with plectrum (all down)

The next thing to try is playing **Exercise 4** now with the plectrum moving down, up, down, up etc.

 Track 10: Exercise 4 with plectrum (down, up, etc.)

How did that go? Are you ready to learn to play the scale of D major?

The D Major Scale

The scale of D major uses both the D and the A string and all the notes we have played so far, with the same fingering as before.

As you have already played all these notes before you should start playing this scale with alternate strokes of the plectrum. This is indicated in the score by the symbols: ⊓ (down-stroke) and ∨ (up-stroke).

Track 11: D Major Scale (i)

It starts on the D string and moves to the A string:

open D string	**D**	down	(⊓)
first finger on D second fret	**E**	up	(∨)
second finger on D fourth fret	**F♯**	down	(⊓)
third finger on D fifth fret	**G**	up	(∨)
open A string	**A**	down	(⊓)
first finger on A second fret	**B**	up	(∨)
second finger on A fourth fret	**C♯**	down	(⊓)
third finger on A fifth fret	**D'**	up	(∨)

Next you can try playing the following in the same way:

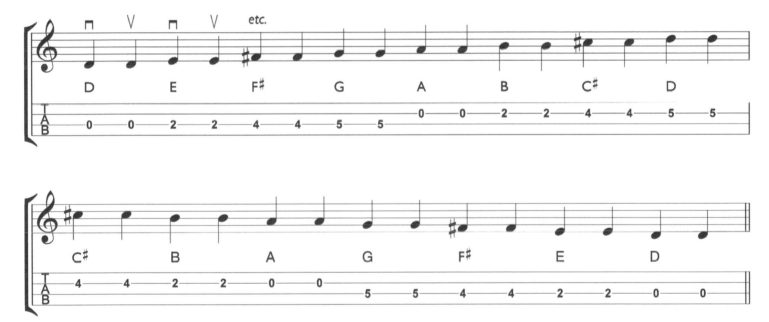

 Track 12: D Major Scale (ii)

Next you can try playing a down-stroke and an up-stroke on each note:

 Track 13: D Major Scale (iii)

You should practise, practise, practise - or more correctly play, play, play - until you can do them without thinking - it's maybe a little tough but you know what I mean!

This leads directly onto learning your first TUNE!

Rhythm

Some Basic Time Signatures

Before moving on to learning our first tunes – armed with our D major scale – we will explain the differences between rhythm and basic time signatures related to Irish music.

The rhythm of a tune determines its time signature, which corresponds to how many notes in a bar of that tune when it is notated. For more information, see the Appendix on the download card.

The tune below, 'My Love Is In America', is a reel. It has four beats (quarter notes) to a bar and its time signature is written as being in 4/4, where each individual note is an eighth note (worth half a beat). A reel is also referred to as being in "common time".

Listen to both versions of the tune, and try to follow the music on the page as the music plays. You'll hear that there is a distinctive "lilt" in the rhythm of the music; a characteristic quality of Irish music.

 Track 14: My Love Is In America
slow tempo; unaccompanied

 Track 15: My Love Is In America
medium tempo; accompanied

My Love Is In America

Trad. arr Éamonn Coyne

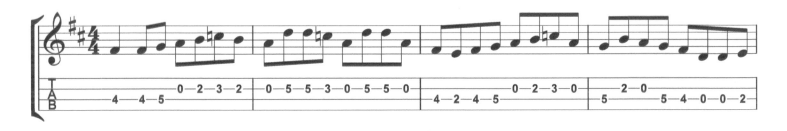

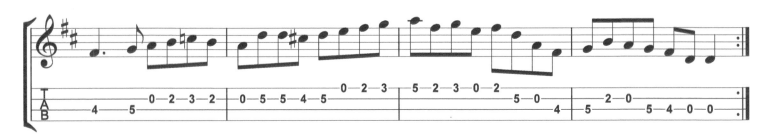

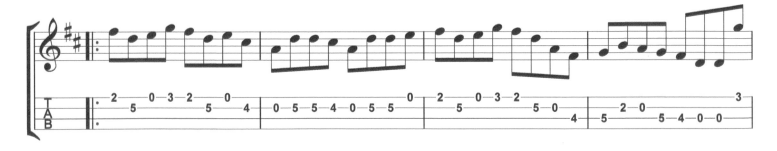

Other common rhythms in Irish music are *jigs*, *slip jigs*, *hornpipes*, *polkas*, *slides*, *marches*, *barndances*, and *waltzes*; however, *reels* are easily the most common.

Reels have four beats to the bar (eight eighth notes) and so the time signature is **4/4**

Jigs have six eighth notes to the bar and so the time signature is **6/8**

Slip Jigs have nine eighth notes to the bar and are written as being in **9/8**

Hornpipes have four beats to the bar and are written in **4/4**

Polkas are written in **2/4**

Slides are written in **12/8**

Marches are commonly written in **2/4** but can be in many time signatures.

Barndances are written in **4/4**

Waltzes are written in **3/4**

▼ The tenor banjo has become quite commonplace in Irish music sessions

Oh! Susanna

Now it's time to try some tunes using the notes you have learned so far.

Oh! Susanna
This starts with the open D (third) string and even though the rhythm isn't totally straight (meaning the notes aren't all rhythmically even – sometimes called a dotted rhythm), you should be able to pick out the tune pretty easily as it is so familiar to us all.

Remember to play all the notes with alternate (down, up) strokes.

Even if you don't read any kind of music and play all the notes straight, you will at least learn where these notes are on the fretboard and the rhythm will come in time with practice.

 Track 16: Oh! Susanna slow tempo

 Track 17: Oh! Susanna medium tempo

 Track 18: Oh! Susanna fast tempo

Oh! Susanna

Stephen Foster (1826-1864)

Because I didn't read staff notation when I was learning the banjo, I would have learnt the rhythm of the tune by ear with the notes written down using a system referred to as ABC notation.

I recommend you learn to read staff notation as it is by far the most commonly used notation system in all forms of music – not only Irish music – and it will keep you on the correct path for the future. However, we've included an appendix to this book to access using the download card which tells you more about this alternative system.

Egan's Polka (*sometimes called the Kerry Polka*) in G
This is a traditional Irish tune from County Kerry, commonly associated with accordion and fiddle, that also uses the D and A strings (although it is more commonly played in a different key – D major – but transposed here for teaching purposes). It is the first tune I learnt!

Something to note here which is very common in Irish music: each section is repeated as signified by the **repeat** barline:

Track 19: Egan's Polka slow tempo

Track 20: Egan's Polka medium tempo

Track 21: Egan's Polka fast tempo

Egan's Polka

Trad. arr Éamonn Coyne

As with 'Oh! Susanna', the same applies to this tune for the notes and rhythm – learn the notes first and the rhythm will come as the tune goes into your head.

Don't forget to play the notes with alternate strokes (starting with a down-stroke).

Note: A polka is played with a 'lift' and that 'lift' is somewhat captured – but maybe not fully – by the dotted notes in the score.

Now let's try some more strings…

The E String

This will be the same as for the other strings but now with an extra note added, played with your fourth finger. Again all notes should be played down, up etc.

On the E string we will play the notes of the key of A. The notes are:

E

open E (first) string

F#'

first finger
on second fret

G#'

second finger
on fourth fret

A'

third finger
on fifth fret

B'

fourth finger
on seventh fret

Exercise 5

 Track 22: Exercise 5

Now you can try playing **Exercise 6**:

Use the same fingers on the way back down to the E, and alternate picking starting with a down-stroke.

 Track 23: Exercise 6

Getting the little finger to play the B' is one of the hardest fingering things you will do for now but it is important to keep working at it. My left thumb moves slightly from its anchor position to play the B'.

How did that go? Are you ready to learn to play some more tunes?

This is a simple but lovely jig from the Sliabh Luachra area of Ireland in the key of A and it uses the E (first) and A (second) strings.

 Track 24: Johnny Leary's slow tempo

 Track 25: Johnny Leary's medium tempo with accompaniment

Johnny Leary's

Trad. arr Éamonn Coyne

This will start you thinking about the idea of playing different notes for different keys. This jig is in the key of A which means it has three sharps: C♯, F♯, and G♯, (although G♯ doesn't actually appear in this piece.)

Again, each part is played twice. Also note the time signature of this tune; a jig is in 6/8. With the two bars at the end; play the 1st time bar and return to the third line, then play the 2nd time bar to finish.

The Rolling Waves

This is another Irish jig but it is in the key of D (which I also recorded in G with Kris Drever on my CD *Honk Toot Suite*, but more of that later) and it uses the E (first), A (second) and D (third) strings. It was probably originally a tune associated with the Uilleann pipes and these often make fine tenor banjo tunes. Because it is in D you will notice that there are two sharps: C# and F#.

Track 26: The Rolling Waves
medium tempo; unaccompanied

Track 27: The Rolling Waves
medium fast tempo; accompanied

The Rolling Waves

Trad. arr Éamonn Coyne

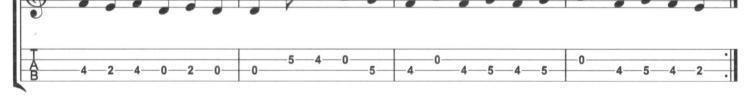

Remember to play each consecutive note with a different stroke (down, up, down *etc.*).

Now we will play the scale of G which is played across three strings: D, A, and E. This scale also introduces the playing of a C (C natural) instead of a C♯, as the key of G has only one sharp: F♯. You should start playing this scale with alternate strokes: down, up, down etc.

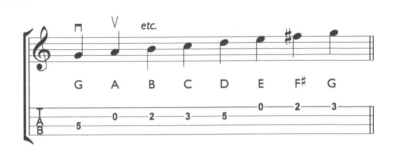

 Track 28: G Major Scale (i)

G
third finger on the fifth fret of the D string

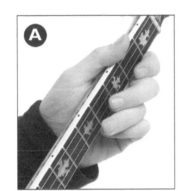

A
open A string

B
first finger on A second fret

C
second finger on A third fret

D'
third finger on A fifth fret

E'
open E string

F♯
first finger on E second fret

G'
second finger on E third fret

Next you can try playing this in the same way:

 Track 29: G Major Scale (ii)

Next you can try playing each note with a down, up stroke so you will play:

 Track 30: G Major scale (iii)

The Ashplant

This is the first reel of the book and it's in the key of E minor which, as it is the *relative minor* of G, it has one sharp: F♯. As it's a reel, it has a time signature of 4/4, often called common time.

As with other tunes in this book, it is my version of a traditional Irish tune. Other versions may differ, perhaps depending on where it was learnt or what instrument was used, but they will all have the basic tune in common.

Up to now each part of a tune has had eight bars, repeated when indicated by a repeat barline :‖ .

However, as is commonly the case in some simpler Irish tunes, the first and fifth bars, and second and sixth bars of the first (and often second) half are the same. Therefore it can be written with the indicators for different part endings on the repeat as is signified by the "1" and "2" over the third and seventh bars of

the first part. The same is also true for the second part of this tune. Of course it could also be written out fully; we keep it as shown for tuition purposes.

By the way, an *ashplant* is a sapling or small branch of an ash tree that was used as a walking stick and also to 'shoo' along the cattle.

Don't forget your down, up etc. on alternate notes. The **Fine** marking means you should stop playing at the last time through. (i.e. on the 'A'.)

 Track 31: The Ashplant
slow tempo; unaccompanied

 Track 32: The Ashplant
medium fast tempo; accompanied

The Ashplant

Trad. arr Éamonn Coyne

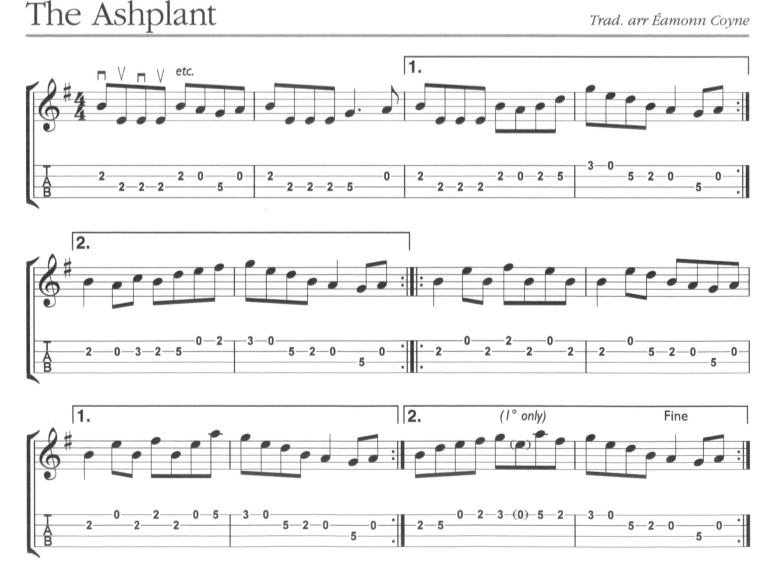

This is a jig in the key of G with a B' (played with your fourth finger on the seventh fret of the E string). It is a very common Irish jig.

Note that because it is in G it has only one sharp (F♯) and has a C♮ (natural) rather than a C♯. Also don't forget to play all consecutive notes down, up. etc.

Track 33: The Kesh
slow tempo; unaccompanied

Track 34: The Kesh
medium fast tempo; accompanied

The Kesh

Trad. arr Éamonn Coyne

Even though overall this is quite an easy tune, the B' in the last bar is awkward and you will probably find that you will have to play it over and over to get it up to speed with the rest of the tune. A trick here is to practise the last two bars together over and over to get the flow right.

Also, if you find it too difficult to land back on the last notes with your second finger, try playing them with your first finger instead (see picture). This is known as *second position* by violinists.

The G String

We will now go to the low and most 'tenor banjo sounding' of all strings: the G (fourth) string. This gives us the following notes when we are playing in the key of G:

Track 35: Exercise 7

G₁
open G (fourth) string

A₁
first finger on second fret

B₁
second finger on fourth fret

C₁
third finger on fifth fret

Now try it up the neck then down again and remember to keep all the strokes down, up etc.:

Track 36: Exercise 8

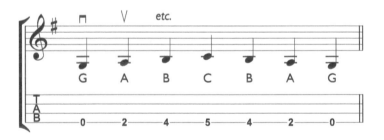

So far we have learned to play the scale of D across two strings – the D and A string (one octave), and the scale of G played across three strings – the third, second, and first strings: D, A, and E. Now try the scale of G across two octaves starting with the fourth string and playing right through the third, second and first strings – the G, D, A, and E strings. It starts with the open G string (G₁) and moves all the way to the second finger on the third fret of the E string (G'):

This is as follows (again, concentrate here on the alternate down – up – down strokes):

open G (fourth) string	**G,**	down	(⊓)
first finger on second fret	**A,**	up	(∨)
second finger on fourth fret	**B,**	down	(⊓)
third finger on fifth fret	**C,**	up	(∨)
open D (third) string	**D**	down	(⊓)
first finger on second fret	**E**	up	(∨)
second finger on fourth fret	**F♯**	down	(⊓)
third finger on fifth fret	**G**	up	(∨)
open A (second) string	**A**	down	(⊓)
first finger on second fret	**B**	up	(∨)
second finger on third fret	**C**	down	(⊓)
third finger on fifth fret	**D'**	up	(∨)
open E (first) string	**E'**	down	(⊓)
first finger on second fret	**F♯'**	up	(∨)
second finger on third fret	**G'**	down	(⊓)

 Track 37: G Major Scale (iv)

Next you can try playing the following in the same way:

 Track 38: G Major Scale (v)

It looks hard, but it is only going up two scales then down again when you reach the top G (G').

You should practise this until you can play it without thinking about it! It will really help your right hand with the flow of the notes (down, up, down) and your left hand for finger positioning (as it uses both the third and fourth frets in there: F♯ on the fourth fret of the D string and C on the third fret of the A string).

This of course leads on to some more TUNES using that wonderful sounding G string.

G Major Scale

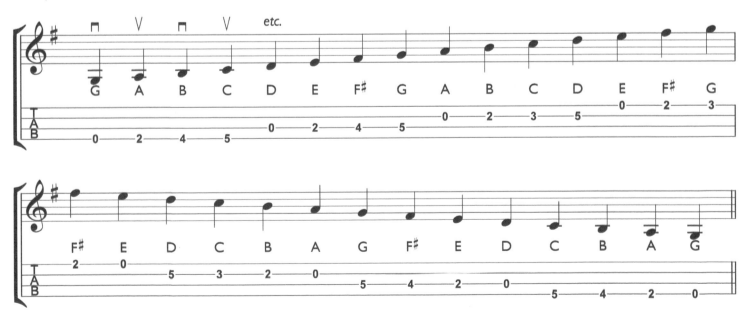

Kitty's Wedding

This is our first hornpipe and it's a lovely tune on the banjo which takes in all four strings with a range B♭ to B'.

A few things to note in the music here:

- It is in the key of D so there are two sharps: C♯ and F♯.
- It has four beats to the bar so it is in 4/4.
- There are two "lead-in" (or "pick-up") notes to each part before the first beat (beat 1).

Track 39: Kitty's Wedding
slow tempo; unaccompanied

Track 40: Kitty's Wedding
medium tempo; accompanied

As it's a hornpipe it is meant to be played slowly with a 'lilt' to it. Don't forget to keep your picking smooth and play all alternate notes down, up etc.; it will flow much better that way.

Kitty's Wedding

Trad. arr Éamonn Coyne

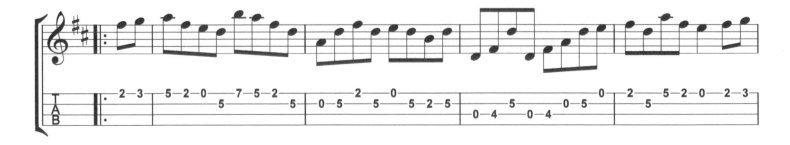

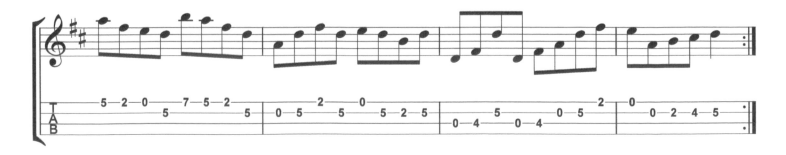

This is a version of a well-known Irish jig. There is a more common version in Am which is a little different but it doesn't have the lovely low A notes, which sound great on the banjo.

Again, a few things to note in the music here:

- It is in the key of E minor (relative minor of G major) so there is only one sharp: F♯.
- It is a jig, so it is in 6/8 time.

Track 41: The Cliffs Of Moher
slow tempo; unaccompanied

Track 42: The Cliffs Of Moher
medium tempo; accompanied

The Cliffs Of Moher

Trad. arr Éamonn Coyne

Ornamentation

What is Ornamentation?

So far, we've looked at playing some tunes exactly as written down. However, an integral part of Irish music is that the players improvise their own embellishments - or ornaments - adding their personal voice to the tunes.

The Triplet

The most common type of ornamentation used on the banjo is the triplet. However, there are many types of triplets and often the tune (and sometimes the type of tune) dictates which one is used and how it is used.

A triplet is three notes (down, up, down), and could be described as putting in three notes in the space of two notes; i.e., a triplet replaces two eighth notes over one beat.

So for a triplet on an A note we could convert an A quarter note or two A eighth notes and get:

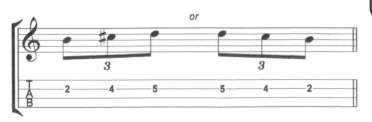

A lot of banjo players will use the former as the way they would play a triplet; I use the latter which I refer to as a two-note triplet instead of a one-note triplet.

I often play another slightly different two-note triplet:

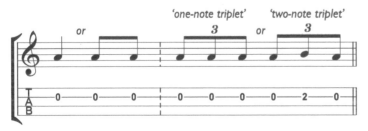

Three-note triplets also exist:

All this makes a lot more sense when using a tune as an example, so we will soon get into the fun part of adding ornamentation to some of the tunes we have learned.

 Track 43: one and two-note triplets starting on A

 Track 44: two-note triplets starting on A

 Track 45: three-note triplets starting on B

Other banjo ornaments include **double stops**, which can be described as playing two notes on different strings together. For example, playing a D (open D string) together with a D' (fifth fret on the A string) gives a drone effect, which can be quite useful for filling out slower tunes. Here are five different double stops (or chords) you can try.

Track 46: five different double stops

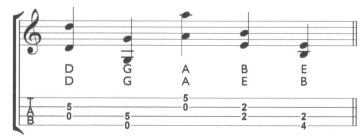

▲ Playing the low double-stop: (B/E)

▲ Playing the medium double-stop: (E/B)

Other ornaments used on the tenor banjo include pull-offs, slides (either up or down the neck), hammer-ons and bending strings, although the latter two are not so common.

For a pull-off the right hand picks a note and you release a left-hand finger — either to an open string, or to an adjacent lower note — at the same time.

For a hammer-on you play a note with the right hand, and then add a finger of the left hand to the fretboard — it's not as common on the banjo as on the guitar but it has its uses.

Slides (generally more common going up the neck on the banjo) are often used in conjunction with double stops e.g. sliding from the high D or D♯ to the E on the A string and playing the E string at the same time. I use the last two types of ornaments in the medleys I play at the end of the book. See if can you spot them!

Tunes with Ornamentation

Johnny Leary's
This simple jig doesn't need much ornamentation and as such is a good introduction to the triplet. As with all tunes there are nearly infinite possibilities for where we add ornamentation, but for simplicity we will add one triplet to each line for starters.

I play all triplets down, up, down with middle note of the various types of triplets (two types shown here) played more softly than the other two (almost muted/dampened).

Track 47: Johnny Leary's (with ornamentation)

Listening to the audio gives you an idea of how triplets are played - with a 'lilt'. You'll get the hang of it after a few listens.

Johnny Leary's

Trad. arr Éamonn Coyne

The Rolling Waves

As with the previous jig, there are lots of ornamentation possibilities with this one. I have shown a few, again, keeping one to a line for simplicity.

Remember that each note of the triplet has a different stroke (down, up, down) and I always start the triplet on a down-stroke. However, I don't always stick to this rule for the notes following the triplet. Often I will play the note following a triplet with a down-stroke as well; e.g., down, up, down, down, especially when moving across strings. This sounds complicated, but try it and you will see what I mean.

Track 48: The Rolling Waves (with ornamentation)

Also, you will note that the last bar of each line in this tune is the same so the triplet I have added in bar 4 on the first line can easily be used in bar 8 or 12 or 16 – however, personally I would not use them in all bars all the time!

The Rolling Waves

Trad. arr Éamonn Coyne

Tunes with Ornamentation and Variations

The Ashplant

I have added some typical triplets for this tune, and even though it's a reel you will note that the ornaments are the same type as we use in jigs. Please remember that not all the ornaments are played each time a part is repeated e.g. I will often play a triplet in bar 3 but nothing or possibly a different ornament on the repeat i.e. in bar 11.

This is indeed true for the repeat of the whole tune; ornaments and variations are just that – different every time!

Track 49: The Ashplant (with ornamentation)

The Ashplant

Trad. arr Éamonn Coyne

The Kesh

Here's another jig and more triplets, which could really appear anywhere in the tune. The first triplet I use (in bar 3) is one which I use pretty commonly in my music: instead of playing a triplet on D (high D) as DDD, I play it as DED, where the E is played  on the seventh fret of the A string with the fourth (little) finger (see photo). The E is not that audible really as it is the semi-muted middle note of the triplet. With practice this becomes second nature. I have also added a couple of other tricks here that I use which are called **variations**.

The first of these is a double stop on the last G in bar 8, where I play a G, (low G) with a G – as with the middle note of a triplet I play this G "chord" softly;

both notes are played with a down-stroke. Of course, this G double stop could be played at the start of the repeat of the first part of the tune too.

The variation I play is in bar 14 involves playing a C♯ in a tune in the key of G, which normally has a C natural. Here this C♯ is known as an accidental. You could also play it instead of the 5th quaver in bar 13, and elsewhere too.

We need to remind ourselves that these ornaments and variations are only played sporadically and usually not in the same place over and over again, so the staff notation is only an approximation of what I do!

 Track 50: The Kesh (with ornamentation)

The Kesh

Trad. arr Éamonn Coyne

Kitty's Wedding

Here are some ornamentations and variations for Kitty's Wedding – I have written the first half out fully to show that different ornaments and variations can be played on the repeats of each part.

Track 51: Kitty's Wedding (with ornamentation)

Kitty's Wedding

Trad. arr Éamonn Coyne

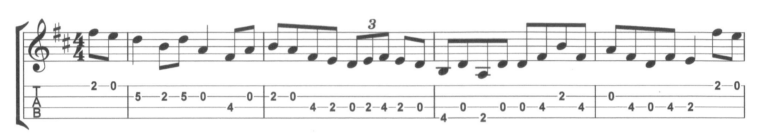

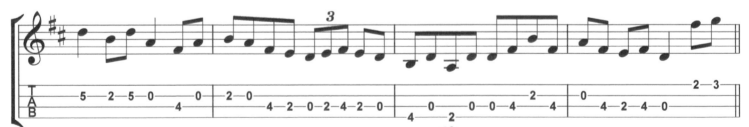

The Cliffs Of Moher

Here are a few more jig triplets to try and practise. There's also a double stop/chord in the last bar which should be played gently and with restraint. This tune is all about the sound of the full range of the banjo coming through and it takes ornamentation but especially variation well. The chord is a combination of the last two on page 35.

Track 52: The Cliffs Of Moher with ornamentation

The Cliffs Of Moher

Trad. arr Éamonn Coyne

My Love Is In America

This reel was the tune from the start of the book which we used as an example of time signatures. It is an interesting tune in that it shows something which is pretty common in Irish music: it is written here in the key of D but it has accidentals built into the tune without them being variations – this is very common in Irish uilleann pipe tunes.

I have written this out fully with no repeats (compare it to that on page 20) to show just how many different options are available when adding ornamentation and variations to a tune – every line in a part can be different even though each part is essentially just repeated.

I have added lots of different types of triplets here – all played the same way, down, up, down, with the middle note slightly muted.

All that said I always like to start a tune with minimal ornamentation and variation and build it up and that is what I have tried to show in this arrangement.

Track 53: My Love Is In America
(with ornamentation)

My Love Is In America

Trad. arr Éamonn Coyne

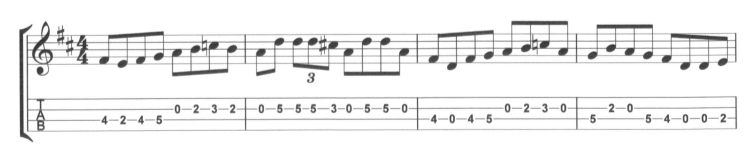

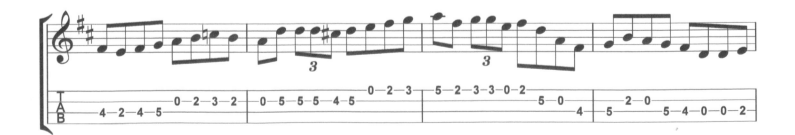

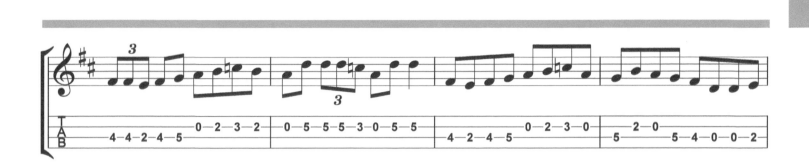

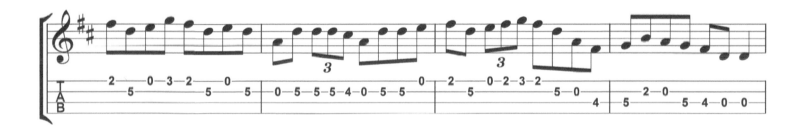

Taking Your Playing Further

What we have learnt, how to get involved in playing, etc.

- We have been introduced to the tenor banjo and its history; what it looks like and its parts; how to hold it and what fingers to put where.

- We have been introduced to various types of notation for tunes (staff, tablature and ABC); various tune rhythms; various types of ornamentation and variations which we can employ to make tunes more interesting to play.

- We have done all this pictorially and by using various types of (predominantly Irish) tunes as examples, nine in total.

This is where we will stop in this book but is not where you should stop. Notated music is readily available from many sources (see below) and I see your next step to be the application of the knowledge learned in this book to different tunes you find from these sources. One of the more interesting things about the notation of Irish and Scottish music (and other types of folk music) is that they are commonly available in their simplest form. It is down to the individual player to add their own ornamentation to these tunes as they see fit – the possibilities are endless. Your next step is to learn as many tunes as you like adding as much ornamentation as you like. But my preference will always be to treat the tune gently when it comes to ornamentation – every instrument can then play together nicely and harmoniously!

Now it's down to you with the motto "Play, Play, Play" with your new partner: the tenor banjo.

To help you on your way I have also added some medleys of the tunes we have learnt. This is by far the most common way tunes are played in the Irish and Scottish music tradition – putting harmoniously matching tunes together in "sets" or "medleys". I don't hold back with ornamentation or variations here and I have not transcribed them so you will just have to try and figure out what I do!

 Track 54: Medley of The Cliffs of Moher, The Kesh, Johnny Leary's and The Rolling Waves

 Track 55: Medley of Kitty's Wedding with My Love Is In America and The Ashplant

If you're feeling particularly adventurous, we've also included the audio to just the guitar parts of the ornamented tracks, so you can practise playing along. These versions are on the download card from track 56 onwards.

This list could go on forever but suffice to say that listening to anything and everything is key – that's what I did. These are some banjo-centric recordings to look out for (listed alphabetically but starting with the papa bear himself Barney McKenna) and is of course, by no means, comprehensive:

Anything that the late great **Barney McKenna** (of the Dubliners and beyond) has recorded – it might not be as technically brilliant in his later years but the soul is what it's all about.

Angelina Carberry has a few recordings out in different guises. Her choice of tunes and, at first-listen, disarmingly simple style makes her an engaging source.

Any of **John Carty**'s CDs (solo or with his band At the Racket) – he has many and nearly always plays a few tunes on banjo or tenor guitar (as well as fiddle and flute!).

Seamus Egan, a multi-instrumentalist from the United States, presents a beautifully in-control ornamented style of banjo playing on his many recordings, either solo or with Solas.

The relatively elusive **Kevin Griffin** is a great player from a great tradition. He has solo recordings (starting with *Traditional Music From Doolin, Co. Clare*) and also some great recordings with The Céilí Bandits.

Kieran Hanrahan recorded many albums with Stockton's Wing and left his great solo album (*Kieran Hanrahan plays the Irish Tenor Banjo*) for a few years later!

Cathal Hayden & Arty McGlynn on *Handed Down*. Cathal is a great banjo and fiddle player and Arty a great guitar accompanist and tune player. This was a seminal album but sits among many other great recordings of theirs.

Brian McGrath, from Fermanagh, who grew up playing with the aforementioned Cathal, has also made some lovely recordings over the years.

Anything you can find by the great **Mick O'Connor** from London is worth hunting out – or just go find him in person playing in sessions around London.

All of **Gerry O'Connor**'s CDs are worth listening to even if his tuning is not for you (CGDA). His control of the instrument and melody is great.

Some early De Dannan albums featured **Charlie Piggot** on banjo and are well worth finding for his great harmonious rhythmic style, especially on *The Mist-Covered Mountain*.

Enda Scahill has made many CDs in different guises over the years and his technique and choice of good banjo tunes is great.

Lastly, anything by the great **Joe Molloy** from Birmingham, who now lives in Dublin—that is if you can find anything. Without hearing Joe play, my life wouldn't be the same.

▼ Barney McKenna

About the Author

Éamonn Coyne (www.eamonncoyne.com), who now lives in Edinburgh, is originally from Ireland (Dublin/Roscommon). His debut solo album *Through the Round Window*, on Compass Records, was released in late 2002. It is a work of banjo music and more, featuring Éamonn on tenor banjo, mandolin, tenor guitar, 6-string guitar and tenor National steel guitar. Accompanying him on the album are a host of luminaries of the Irish music scene and beyond, including: Grammy award-winner Alison Brown, (5-string banjo), from California via Nashville; Dermot Byrne (accordion and melodeon) and Ciarán Curran (bouzouki), both of Altan; Kevin Doherty (guitar and vocals) of Four Men and a Dog; Michael McGoldrick (flute) of Capercaille & the Mark Knopfler Band; and Tom Morrow (fiddle) of Dervish. *fRoots* called it "utterly stunning" and *The Irish Times* reported, "… this album comes as no surprise either in its virtuosity or eclecticism".

Coyne has also performed and recorded with a vast array of people including Siobhán and Tommy Peoples, The Wrigley Sisters (CDs *Huldreland*, *Mither o' the Sea*, and *Idiom*), Eileen Ivers (ex-Riverdance), Sharon Shannon, piper Allan MacDonald, Bèla Fleck, Jerry Douglas, Sinéad O'Connor, Tim O'Brien, and Russell's House (CD *Russell's House*). Éamonn currently tours and records with Scottish 'international' band Salsa Celtica (CDs *El Agua de la Vida*, *El Camino*, *En Vivo en el Norte*, and 2014's *The Tall Islands*). He also plays with new supergroup Treacherous Orchestra, whose debut album *Origins* was released to critical acclaim in 2012 and 2015's follow-up, *Grind*, is on a similar trajectory.

He also regularly tours with multi-instrumentalist and vocalist Kris Drever, and their CD *Honk Toot Suite*, was released in 2007, again on Compass Records. *Songlines* described it as "a breath of fresh air" with its "mutually attuned musicianship of the first order" and "its immense yet ultra-supple sophistication". The duo's most recent album *Storymap*, released in 2013 on Reveal Records, has also received widespread critical acclaim, including *BBC Music Magazine*'s Album of the Month in September 2013 with a five-star review.

Wrigley Sisters	**Huldreland**	1996	Greentrax Recordings
Wrigley Sisters	**Mither o' the Sea**	1999	Greentrax Recordings
Various Artists incl. Russell's House	**Folkal Point: Edinburgh**	1999	Greentrax Recordings
Russell's House	**Russell's House**	1999	Atcof Music
Jonny Hardie & Gavin Marwick	**The Blue Lamp**	1999	Lochshore
Wrigley Sisters	**Skyran**	2001	GS
Éamonn Coyne	**Through the Round Window**	2002	Compass Records
Salsa Celtica	**El Agua de la Vida**	2003	Greentrax Recordings
Salsa Celtica	**El Camino**	2006	Discos León
Éamonn Coyne & Kris Drever	**Honk Toot Suite**	2007	Compass Records
Various Artists incl. Allan MacDonald and Kris Drever	**A Celebration of the Music of Gordon Duncan A National Treasure**	2007	Greentrax Recordings
Various Artists incl. Alison Brown Quartet and Kris Drever	**Wells for Zoë – Water for Life**	2009	Compass Records
Treacherous Orchestra	**EP**	2009	Takit
Salsa Celtica	**En Vivo en el Norte**	2010	Discos León
Wrigley Sisters	**Idiom**	2011	GS
Kris Drever's Band	**EP**	2012	Reveal Records
Treacherous Orchestra	**Origins**	2012	Navigator Records
Éamonn Coyne & Kris Drever	**Storymap**	2013	Reveal Records (ROW) & Compass Records (Americas)
Salsa Celtica	**The Tall Islands**	2014	Discos León
Kris Drever & Éamonn Coyne	**Mareel EP**	2014	Reveal Records
Treacherous Orchestra	**Grind**	2015	Reveal Records